WELCOME TO LIBYA

COUNTRIES OF THE WORLD

Libya

by Kevin Kurtz

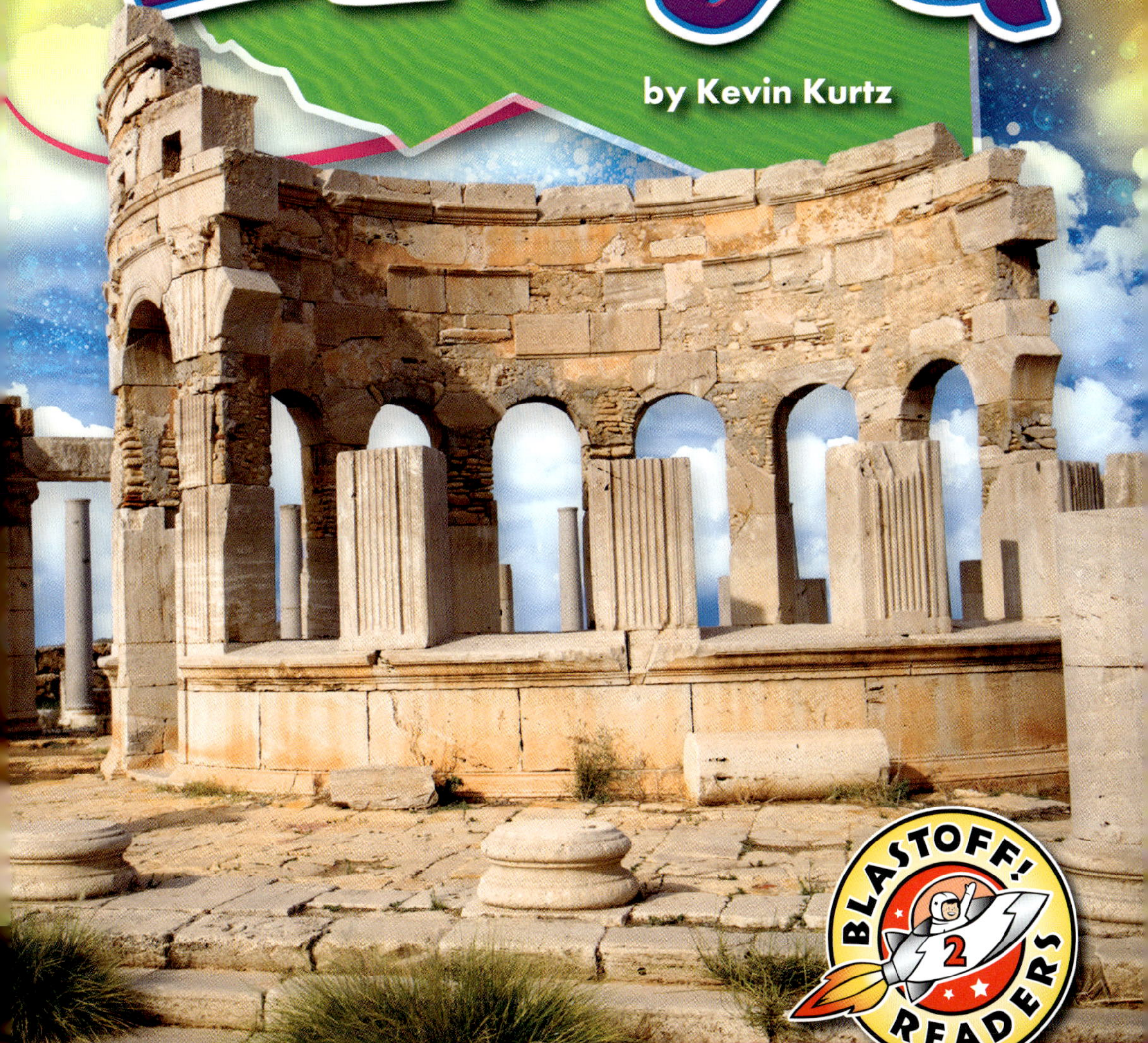

BLASTOFF! READERS 2

BLASTOFF! READERS, AN IMPRINT OF BELLWETHER MEDIA BY FLUTTERBEE

Blastoff! Readers are carefully developed by literacy experts to build reading stamina and move students toward fluency by combining standards-based content with developmentally appropriate text.

LEVELS

Level 1 provides the most support through repetition of high-frequency words, light text, predictable sentence patterns, and strong visual support.

Level 2 offers early readers a bit more challenge through varied sentences, increased text load, and text-supportive special features.

Level 3 advances early-fluent readers toward fluency through increased text load, less reliance on photos, advancing concepts, longer sentences, and more complex special features.

★ **Blastoff! Universe**

This edition first published in 2027 by Bellwether Media, Inc.

For information regarding permission, write to Bellwether Media, Inc., Attention: Permissions Department, 3500 American Blvd W, Suite 150, Bloomington, MN 55431.

Library of Congress Cataloging-in-Publication Data

Names: Kurtz, Kevin author
Title: Libya / Kevin Kurtz. Other titles: Blastoff! readers. 2 Countries of the world
Description: Blastoff! readers. | Minneapolis : Bellwether Media, Inc, 2026. | Series: Blastoff! readers. Countries of the world | Includes bibliographical references and index. | Audience: Ages 5-8 | Audience: Grades 2-3 | Summary: "Relevant images match informative text in this introduction to Libya. Intended for students in kindergarten through third grade"–Provided by publisher.
Identifiers: LCCN 2026010678 (print) | LCCN 2026010679 (ebook) | ISBN 9798898800468 library binding | ISBN 9798898801700 ebook Subjects: LCSH: Libya
Classification: LCC DT215 .K87 2026 (print) | LCC DT215 (ebook) | DDC 961.2-dc23/eng/20260219
LC record available at https://lccn.loc.gov/2026010678
LC ebook record available at https://lccn.loc.gov/2026010679

Editor: Betsy Rathburn Designer: Laura Sowers

Printed in the United States of America, North Mankato, MN.

Table of Contents

All About Libya

Libya is a big country in North Africa. Its capital city is Tripoli.

Libya has many old **ruins**. The city of Cyrene is over 2,500 years old.

Land and Animals

The Sahara **Desert** covers most of Libya. **Oases** dot the desert.

Beaches line the coast along the Mediterranean Sea. Nearby mountains are green with plants.

oasis

Acacus Mountains

Size: tallest arch is 492 feet (150 meters) tall

Famous For: rock art that is up to 14,000 years old

Libya is hot and dry. Some areas go without rain for years.

Sand covers most of Libya. **Sandstorms** blow sand through the air.

Fat-tailed gerbils sleep in desert holes. Fennec foxes hunt for them.

loggerhead sea turtle

Animals of Libya

fat-tailed gerbil

fennec fox

desert horned viper

loggerhead sea turtle

Horned vipers creep through desert sand. Loggerhead sea turtles lay eggs on beaches.

Life in Libya

Most people in Libya are **Arabs**. The main language is Arabic.

Islam is the most common religion. Almost all Libyans live in cities on the coast.

English: Hello

Arabic: Marhaban

(mar-HAB-ahn)

soccer

The most popular sport is soccer. Some people watch horse races.

People love visiting family and friends. They also enjoy picnics and going to the beach.

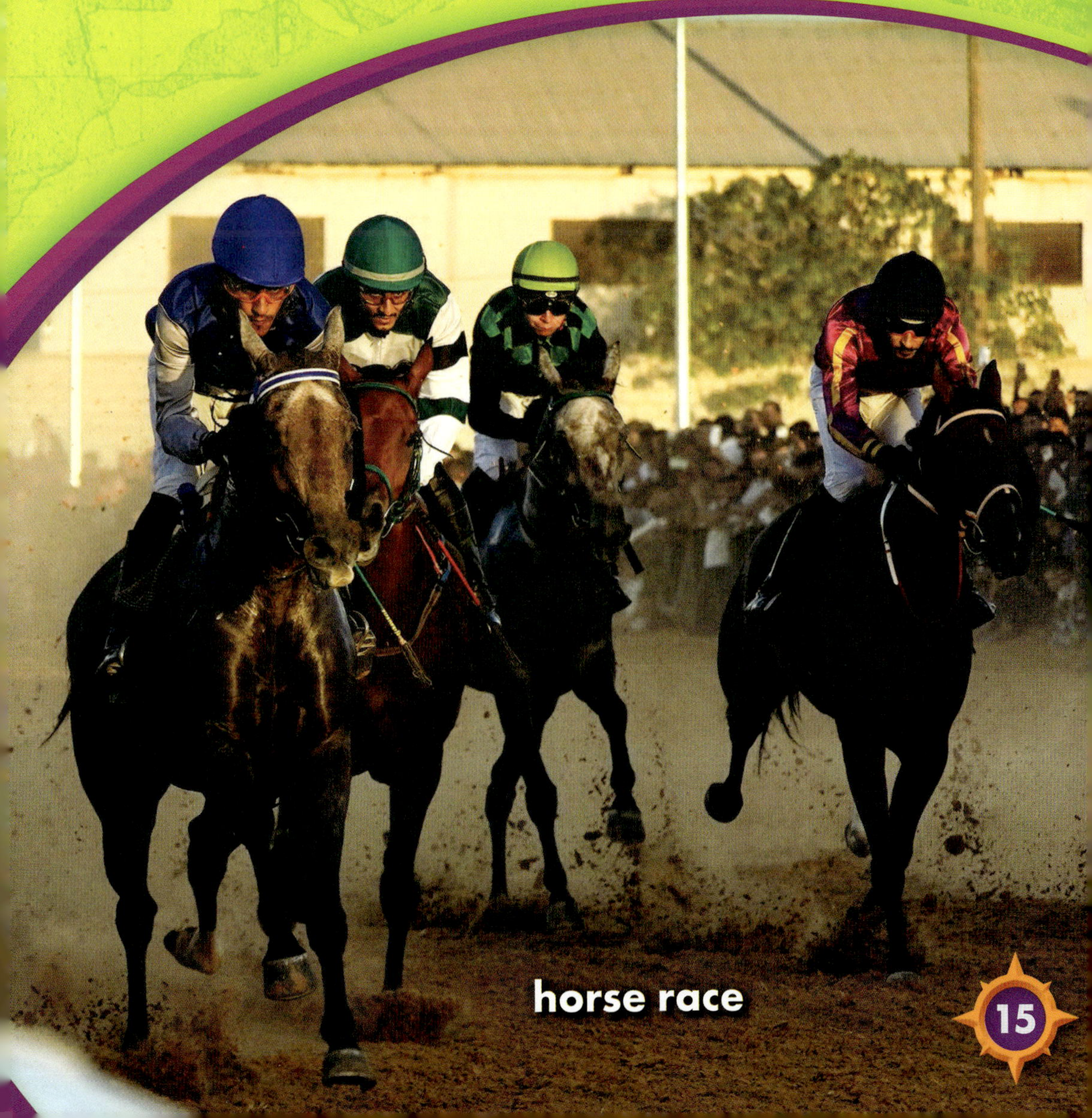

horse race

Magrood are cookies filled with **dates**. *Mbakbaka* is a spicy pasta.

Libyan Foods

magrood

mbakbaka

couscous

sharba

Couscous is often served with vegetables and lamb. *Sharba* is a soup made with lamb and spices.

Eid al-Fitr is a big holiday. **Muslims** pray and enjoy a feast.

The Ghat **Festival** honors Amazigh **culture**. It has camel races, music, and dancing. Libyans love their family, friends, and culture!

Ghat Festival

Eid al-Fitr

Libya Facts

Size:
679,362 square miles
(1,759,540 square kilometers)

Population:
7,361,263 (2024)

National Holidays:
Liberation Day (October 23)
Independence Day (December 24)

Main Language:
Arabic

Capital City:
Tripoli

Famous Face

Name: Moatasem Al-Musrati

Famous For: popular soccer player and captain of Libya's national soccer team

Religions

Top Landmarks

Cyrene

Fezzan oases

Kabaw Fort

Glossary

Arabs—people who live mostly in West Asia and northern Africa

couscous—a type of pasta made from wheat rolled into tiny balls

culture—the beliefs, arts, and ways of life of a place or group of people

dates—sweet fruits that grow on trees

desert—dry land with few plants and little rainfall

festival—a time or event of celebration

Islam—a religion based on belief in Allah as the only God and in Muhammad as God's follower

Muslims—people of the Islamic faith

oases—places in deserts where water is present and plants can grow

ruins—the damaged remains of ancient buildings or other things

sandstorms—events in which very strong winds blow sand around with great force in deserts

To Learn More

AT THE LIBRARY

Gould, Sloane. *Libya*. Buffalo, N.Y.: Cavendish Square Publishing, 2026.

Green, Sara. *Deserts*. Minneapolis, Minn.: Bellwether Media, 2022.

Wilkins, Veronica B. *Explore Africa*. Minneapolis, Minn.: Jump!, 2020.

ON THE WEB

FACTSURFER

Factsurfer.com gives you a safe, fun way to find more information.

1. Go to www.factsurfer.com.
2. Enter "Libya" into the search box and click 🔍.
3. Select your book cover to see a list of related content.

Index

The images in this book are reproduced through the courtesy of: Jason Row Photo, front cover; Robert Harding Video, front cover; TheFlagCompany, p. 3; Hussein Eddeb, pp. 4-5; Marie Young, p. 5; Patrick Poendl, pp. 6, 6-7, 21 (Fezzan oases); Taha Sayeh, pp. 8-9; Marco, p. 9; prochym, pp. 10-11; DS light photography, p. 11 (fat-tailed gerbil); ArtushFoto, p. 11 (fennec fox); Lauren Suryanata, p. 11 (desert horned viper); NaturePicsFilms, p. 11 (loggerhead sea turtle); Imago/ Alamy, p. 12; John Warburton Lee/ Warburton Lee, John/ SuperStock, pp. 12-13; Richard Human/ Alamy, p. 14; Xinhua/ Alamy, pp. 14-15, 18-19; Ahmed Alkmeshi, p. 16 (*magrood*); Dina Saeed, p. 16 (*mbakbaka*); nesavinov, p. 16 (couscous); Fanfo, p. 16 (*sharba*); Charles O. Cecil/ Alamy, p. 17; Bashar Shglila/ Getty Images, p. 18; daboost, p. 20 (flag); ANP/ Alamy, p. 20 (Moatsem Al-Musrati); lapas77, p. 21 (Cyrene); Styve Reineck, p. 21 (Kabaw Fort); Farinoza, p. 22.